Curbing EC2 Instance Credit Balance Exhaustion

Table of Contents

Chapter 1. Introduction

In this Special Report, we delve into the crucial topic of Curbing EC2 Instance Credit Balance Exhaustion. This may seem like a highly technical terrain, but don't fret! We have patiently explained each concept, breaking down intricate jargon into straightforward language. We'll explore the fundamental principles behind AWS's EC2 instances, understand the concept of CPU Credit balance, and most importantly, discuss strategies to prevent its exhaustion. This report will act as your compass, guiding you in the labyrinth of cloud computing, ensuring your operations are efficient, cost-effective, and free of avoidable disruptions. You don't need to be a tech whiz to comprehend; all you need is the interest to optimize your AWS resources. Get ready to unveil strategies that can potentially save you time, money, and enhance your AWS EC2 instances' performance. Unpack complexity, one page at a time!

Chapter 2. Understanding AWS and EC2 Instances

In simple terms, Amazon Web Services (AWS) is a pioneer in offering platforms for secure cloud services, storage, content delivery, and other features to help businesses grow. Many organizations find it a cost-effective, dependable, and innovative platform that aids in developing a robust and scalable environment.

AWS provides numerous services from which organizations can choose based on their requirements. One such service is Amazon's Elastic Compute Cloud (EC2). The EC2 provides scalable computing capacity by giving secure and resizable compute capacity. A broad understanding of this technology can add significant value to your organization's overall cloud strategy.

2.1. Deep Dive into AWS

AWS is an expansive and powerful set of cloud-based services offered by Amazon. The services provided by AWS range from storage solutions to machine learning and artificial intelligence resources. With AWS's help, businesses can leverage quality services with a pay-as-you-go model, which allows them to pay only for what they use, a model which is considered convenient, flexible, and cost-effective.

It's crucial to understand the shared model responsibility that AWS operates with. In this model, AWS is responsible for the security "of" the cloud while organizations have the responsibility for security "in" the cloud. AWS oversees the infrastructure, software, networking, and facilities that run its services. Meanwhile, organizations manage the security configuration and management tasks based on their implementation, specifically concerning their customer data and environment.

2.2. EC2- Elastic Compute Cloud

To slightly pivot our focus, Amazon's Elastic Compute Cloud, better known as EC2, is a service that provides secure and resizable compute capacity in the cloud. It is a major part of the AWS suite, designed to ease computing for developers. The EC2 service eliminates the need for investing in hardware, thereby aiding businesses in developing and delivering applications faster.

EC2 provides a web-based service where developers can requisition compute server instances to run their applications. These server instances are virtual machines that can be configured by the developer to suit their application needs. EC2 offers a wide range of instance types optimized to fit different use cases, basing them on memory, compute capacity, storage, and networking capability.

EC2 instances come in varied types, each designed keeping a particular type of workload in mind. These instance types optimize various combinations of CPU, memory, storage, and networking capacity and provide the flexibility to choose the right mix for your workloads.

The beauty of using EC2 lies in two of its key features - scalability and elasticity. When we talk of scalability, we refer to accommodating growth. As an organization's demands grow, more instances can be easily added. Elasticity refers to the need-based usage. When there is a spike in the requirement, more instances can be added, and likewise, they can be released when the demand drops. This makes EC2 an efficient and cost-friendly service.

2.3. CPU Credit Balance in EC2 Instances

While using AWS EC2, particularly the T2 or T3 instances, you may have come across the term 'CPU Credit Balance.' Understanding CPU

Credit Balance is crucial to avoid unexpected charges or performance issues.

CPU Credits in EC2 instances provide the capability of burst performance. In other words, they can enhance the CPU performance during the periods of high demand. Each T2 or T3 instance starts with a CPU Credit balance, and depending upon the instance size, earns (or is given) a certain number of CPU Credits per hour. When an instance needs to burst above the baseline performance (i.e., use more CPU than typically allowed), the instance spends the CPU Credits in its balance.

The CPU Credit balance feature enables instances with lower CPU utilization to accrue credits during inactive periods, which are then consumed during periods of peak demand, leading to better application performance. However, if the CPU Credit balance is exhausted, the CPU burst capacity is throttled, which can lead to slower application performance.

In the following sections, we will explore intricacies of managing and monitoring the CPU Credit balance most effectively, in addition to detailed strategies that'll help prevent its exhaustion, ensuring that your AWS EC2 instances function optimally without any avoidable disruptions.

The understanding of AWS services and EC2 instances underlines the springboard to deriving an effective strategy for preventing CPU Credit Balance exhaustion. This understanding not only helps to create a cost-effective solution but also ensures that there will be no hindrance to performance due to a lack of available CPU credits.

Chapter 3. Unpacking Concepts: CPU, Burstable Performance Instances, and Credit Balance

Let's begin our journey into the realms of cloud computing by unpacking three fundamental concepts: CPU, Burstable Performance Instances, and CPU Credit Balance. We must tear down the veil to see the bare components of these seemingly intimidating terms and understand their workings in layman's terms.

3.1. What is CPU?

The Central Processing Unit (CPU) is the core component or the "brain" of a computer, server, phone, or any computational device. It is responsible for execution of instructions and processes. Most CPUs nowadays have multiple cores, each one capable of processing distinct information independently. For multicore CPUs, think of each core as a separate CPU within the CPU.

This key component carries out tasks such as running operating systems, applications, and reading or writing data. The speed at which a CPU performs these tasks is measured in gigahertz (GHz), which is used to gauge the number of billions of cycles the CPU can handle in one second.

High CPU usage can improve the performance of some tasks like data crunching but can have a negative effect, like slowing down processes, if not managed properly. In other words, controlling CPU usage is as important as having a high-performance one.

3.2. Burstable Performance Instances Explained

Now that we understand what a CPU is and its role in processing tasks, let's explore the concept of Burstable Performance Instances in the context of cloud computing, particularly in Amazon Web Services (AWS).

Burstable Performance Instances are a form of Amazon EC2 instances that are designed to offer a baseline level of CPU performance with the ability to "burst," i.e., to utilize higher levels of CPU power when needed. These instances are an ideal and cost-effective choice for workloads that don't use the full CPU often but occasionally need to burst (i.e., utilize more CPU).

Under the hood, burstable performance instances work in conjunction with CPU Credits. These credits determine the amount and duration of bursting a particular instance can accommodate. Understanding this concept leads us to the final key term for this section – the CPU Credit Balance.

3.3. Deciphering CPU Credit Balance

Each Burstable Performance Instance is equipped with a CPU credit balance. These CPU credits, each representing a measure of CPU performance for a fixed amount of time, are spent when the instance needs to burst and earned when it is idle or using less than baseline performance.

When an instance is created, it gets initial CPU credits and it keeps earning credits every hour, depending on the instance type and size. The earned credits are accumulated in the CPU Credit Balance and can be spent whenever more CPU power is required.

One of the crucial things to understand here is that the CPU credits do expire. If an instance does not consume all earned credits within 24 hours, they will be discarded. This essentially means CPU credits are a "use-it-or-lose-it" resource.

The intricate dance between the need to burst, the production of CPU credits, and the management of the CPU credit balance is what assures optimal performance of AWS resources without incurring unnecessary costs.

3.4. Implications for EC2 Instances

Understanding the interplay of these three critical components - the CPU, Burstable Performance Instances, and the CPU Credit Balance - is crucial for effectively leveraging the burstable nature of EC2 instances.

1. Monitoring: Regularly monitor your CPU utilizations and the CPU credit balance. AWS CloudWatch is a good tool for this. Monitoring will help you understand your instance's performance over time and plan necessary actions to avoid credit balance exhaustion.

2. Right-sizing: Choose the right instance size based on your needs. Larger instances earn more CPU credits per hour than smaller ones, so if your load is intensive, go for the larger ones. But remember, they come with more cost.

3. Expiry considerations: Since the earned credits expire in 24 hours, they must be used strategically. If the CPU does not require to burst, try to maintain the performance below the baseline to stockpile credits for when you might need them more.

4. Reserve Instances: If your workload is predictable and consistent, Reserved Instances might prove more cost-effective. It is essential to carefully assess your needs before opting for this.

5. Set up alerts: AWS provides the ability to set up alerts if CPU usage or credit balance exceeds certain thresholds. Use this

feature to avoid unexpected high bills and ensure your EC2 instances are running efficiently.

Though it may seem an intricate play of concepts and components, with effective monitoring, right-sizing, and anticipating resource usage, you can efficiently manage your EC2 instances so that they balance performance and cost-effectiveness.

Taking the time to understand and apply these concepts will ensure you effectively harness the remarkable capabilities of AWS EC2 instances without worrying about exhausting your CPU credit balance. Consider this knowledge a key tool in your cloud optimization toolkit.

Chapter 4. The Phenomena of EC2 Instance Credit Balance Exhaustion

The game of managing AWS EC2 instances effectively necessitates deep knowledge of the underlying inherent lifecycles and policies attached with these instances. EC2 instance credit balance exhaustion is one such pivotal area that requires careful examination to maintain uninterrupted, cost-effective operation of your cloud-based services.

The crux of the matter lies in comprehending the concept of CPU credit balance and its significance in managing the performance of your EC2 instances. CPU credit balance represents the amount of CPU performance, measured in vCPU-minutes, that your instances can utilize. Burstable performance instances accrue these CPU credits and consume them whenever they operate above their baseline performance.

Understanding the impact of Burst Balancing on your account, and indeed, its role in leading to CPU credit balance exhaustion, is fundamental.

4.1. Burst Balance and its Impact

Burstable performance instances, as the name suggests, are designed to deliver a baseline level of CPU performance and the capability to burst above this baseline when needed. The instances accomplish this bursting with the help of CPU credits that it accrues over time, at a millisecond-level resolution.

Accrued CPU credits allow your instances to burst when necessary, providing extra power to handle workload spikes efficiently. The catch here is, once your instance depletes its CPU credit balance, it can no longer afford to burst, thus restricting its performance to the baseline level. This phenomenon is referred to as EC2 instance credit balance exhaustion.

Observing CPU credit consumption, calculating the burst balance, and appropriately planning the required baseline performance can safeguard against sudden drops in performance due to credit exhaustion.

4.2. Credit Accrual and Depletion

Instances start their life with a full CPU credit balance. They add to this balance each hour at a rate determined by the size of the instance, if it's running at or below the baseline performance level. When the instance requires bursts of power, it consumes from the CPU credit balance.

The rate of consumption is proportional to the amount of CPU usage that exceeds the instance's baseline capacity. If your workload is consistently operating above the baseline throughout the working day, the credit balance can be exhausted very quickly, leading to performance throttling.

Such instances, workloads that require long periods of high CPU usage, are usually better off using fixed performance instances (non-burstable instances).

4.3. Strategies to Prevent Credit Balance Exhaustion

Now that you understand what credit balance exhaustion is and why it happens, let's delve into ways to prevent it.

4.3.1. Monitoring and Alerts

Monitoring CPU credit balance, available via the CloudWatch service, is crucial for efficiently managing CPU performance. Analyzing the CPU credit consumption trends can help identify patterns and predict future credit balance depletion before it hits.

Setting up CloudWatch Alerts to notify when CPU credit balance falls below a certain threshold is a proactive strategy to prevent credit depletion, providing an opportunity to take corrective action before any possible performance degradation.

4.3.2. Vertical Scaling

Instances that consistently exhaust their CPU credit balance might be operating beyond their size capacity. In this situation, upgrading to a larger burstable instance, or switching to a different instance type with a higher baseline performance, can solve the problem. This is typically known as Vertical Scaling.

For example, you might consider scaling from a T2.micro to a T2.medium instance. The T2.medium has a higher CPU credit accumulation rate and a bigger CPU credit bucket, thereby potentially avoiding any credit balance exhaustion.

4.3.3. Horizontal Scaling

Adding more instances is another way to distribute the processing load and maintain an ample CPU credit balance. This process, known as Horizontal Scaling, can help mitigate the threat of a credit balance exhaustion.

Using EC2 Auto Scaling is an effective way to horizontally scale your instances. When CPU credit balances deplete across instances, the Auto Scaling service can spawn new instances, effectively distributing the load, and maintaining a sufficient credit balance.

4.3.4. Utilize Unlimited Mode

T3 and T3a instances offer 'Unlimited Mode', which allows instances to burst beyond the credit limit, even after exhausting the CPU credit balance. While instances in Unlimited Mode can protect against credit balance exhaustion, they may incur additional costs if they operate above their baseline performance for extended periods.

4.4. Conclusion

Performance management and cost-optimization in AWS invariably implies good EC2 instance management. An essential part of this involves understanding and mitigating the risk of CPU credit balance exhaustion.

Through continuous monitoring and alerting, vertical and horizontal scaling, and by leveraging AWS features like Auto Scaling and Unlimited Mode, you can ensure your cloud setup remains robust and efficient, even as demand fluctuates. Most importantly, you'll keep your services running at full throttle, ensuring those relying on them remain contented with your service offerings.

Chapter 5. Implications of Depleted Credit Balance on System Performance

The phenomenon of depleted credit balance in your Amazon EC2 instances is far from being a benign matter. It can create significant short and long term repercussions for your system's performance. Overall drawbacks can be detected in two major areas: operational continuity and cost of services.

5.1. Operational Continuity

A crucial concern when your CPU credit balance dwindles or is exhausted is the impact on operational continuity. When EC2 instances have spent all their CPU credits, their capacity to maintain or increase CPU usage decreases significantly.

Imagine a scenario where your instance has run out of CPU credits and experiences an unexpected, but temporary surge in traffic. In the absence of spare CPU credits, the system's capacity to scale and accommodate this additional use is severely impeded. This could lead to longer response times or, in the worse case scenario, the unavailability of the service.

The performance of your EC2 instances is directly proportional to the available CPU Credit balance. High credit balance allows instances to burst beyond their baseline performance, handling a sudden increase in load efficiently. So, a depleted credit balance equates to a drop in performance, and more critically, issues with service availability.

A more insidious impact is the potential effect on time-critical operations. For operations that demand high CPU input, having an ample credit balance is absolutely essential. The absence of sufficient CPU credits could extend the time required for these operations, causing failures due to timeout errors.

5.2. Cost of Services

Another significant area where a depleted CPU Credit balance impacts an organization is cost. Generally, CPU credits are part of the package when you sign up for T2 or T3 instances; they accrue hourly and can be consumed when needed without any additional charge. This setup allows companies to effectively handle variable workloads without incurring extra costs.

However, when the credits run out, to maintain the required level of performance, you might need to consider upgrading to a larger or unlimited instance. Upgrading to a new instance or switching to unlimited mode will indeed ensure the continuity of services, but it comes with increased costs. The financial impact could be substantial if this needs to be done regularly.

One might consider that letting the service degrade or become unavailable could be a way out, to avoid additional costs. But remember, service disruption could also lead to reputational damage and loss of business, translating into indirect costs.

Alternatively, relying on CPU Credit purchasing to supplement insufficiency can become an expensive affair if not managed properly. Especially in the T3 unlimited mode, you may end up spending way more than planned if your credit balance runs low and consumption rates remain high.

5.3. Performance Degradation Over Time

The impact of a dwindling CPU Credit Balance is not always immediate or apparent. Over time, performance degradation becomes more noticeable, and identifying the root cause may not always be straightforward.

If unmonitored, instances with faltering CPU Credit Balances can lead to a gradual decline in performance. Critical applications may start becoming sluggish, with delayed responses and prolonged execution times. The impact can be subtle at first, only becoming clear when the system performance has degraded to a level that severely affects user experience and business operations.

Instance performance in EC2 is reliant on a delicate equilibrium. If your CPU Credit balance runs dry and you have exhausted your instances' burst capacity, you are essentially left with baseline performance for the instance type that you have chosen. This baseline performance will most likely not cater to your needs if your applications depend on CPU bursts to deliver their full functionality.

5.4. Conclusion

While seemingly a technical detail, managing CPU Credit Balance is of operational and financial significance. Inadequate management can lead to operational disruption and drive up the cost of maintaining your EC2 instances. Moreover, performance degradation is gradual and can go unnoticed until it becomes a significant issue. Careful monitoring and timely management of the CPU credit balance can help ensure smoother operations, avert service disruptions, and control costs effectively.

In the next section, we will be exploring strategies to prevent EC2 instance CPU Credit Balance exhaustion, ensuring that your operation never falls victim to the repercussions of a depleted credit balance.

Chapter 6. Analyzing EC2 Credit Exhaustion: Real-World Cases

Amazon Web Services' Elastic Compute Cloud (EC2) instances are incredibly powerful tools, backed by a balance of CPU Credit that ensures operations run smoothly. However, the control this offers can come with its pitfalls. This chapter will dive into understanding and analyzing EC2 Credit Exhaustion through real-world cases.

6.1. The Burp Suite Case

One critical example of credit exhaustion in AWS's EC2 instance was highlighted by a user running Burp Suite, a software framework for performing security testing of web applications. Burp Suite is known for its intensive computational activities, placing significant load on the CPU.

When launching the Burp Suite on an EC2 t2.medium instance, the user observed that the EC2 instance credit balance was depleting rapidly, impacting the instance performance. The Burp Suite was intensely active during the initial few hours, consuming CPU credits quicker than the instance's accrual rate.

A detailed analysis of CloudWatch metrics revealed that the Burp suite was causing CPU spikes leading to credit exhaustion. To combat this, the user had to ensure that Burp Suite didn't consume all available CPU credits and initiated burst performance only when necessary.

6.2. The Data Mining Application Case

In another scenario, a company running a data mining application on a t2.micro instance found that their instance credit balance was running dry too soon. Their application was on regularly pulling in information from various sources, parsing it, and writing it to a database. This continuous process was causing CPU usage spikes.

On investigating CloudWatch, they noticed that the CPU credit balance was not sufficient to maintain optimal performance. Whenever their application started a new process, large bursts of CPU credits were consumed, degrading the instance's performance.

The solution was to fine-tune the intervals at which the application was pulling in data, parsing it, and writing it to the database. By maintaining a stable rate of operations, CPU credit consumption was minimized, helping the instance to sustain its performance.

6.3. The Shared Environment Case

Shared environments where multiple developers are pulling and pushing codes to EC2 instances is another typical scenario where instances may face premature credit exhaustion. In such cases, every developer might run numerous processes, causing the CPU to be over-utilized and credits to drain rapidly.

A deep dive into CloudWatch metrics showed peaks in CPU usage at specific times, leading to the exhaustion of CPU credit balance. These peaks often coincided with build processes, frequent code pushes, or other intensive tasks.

To prevent credit exhaustion in such scenarios, the team implemented several measures like setting 'pull' and 'push' restrictions during peak hours, performing minor tasks during nonpeak hours, and adopting conservative instance sizes during non-demanding periods.

6.4. The eCommerce Platform Case

A popular eCommerce platform found itself facing instances of EC2 credit exhaustion, particularly during festive seasons when the load on servers would be exceptionally high due to increased user activity and traffic. With sudden and unpredictable surges in CPU usage, there was rapid draining of the CPU credit balance, affecting the server's performance and the user experience.

An examination of CloudWatch metrics revealed that spontaneous traffic spikes were the main cause of CPU credit exhaustion. Instance performance degraded significantly during these peak periods.

To combat this, the eCommerce platform used auto-scaling to manage demand more effectively. Auto-scaling, coupled with load balancing, ensured that the load was distributed equally, preventing any single instance from being overworked and running into CPU credit exhaustion.

These real-life instances underline the importance of actively monitoring CPU usage and EC2 instance credit balance. Whether you run an intensive data processing application, a shared development environment, or a platform with changing loads, preventive strategies and instigating changes based on analytical data should prevent future crises. Above all, an understanding of your application's behavior and its impact on the EC2 instance can help arrest issues of credit exhaustion, ensure smooth instance function, and keep the costs manageable.

Chapter 7. Strategies to Minimize EC2 Instance Credit Exhaustion

The consumption of EC2 instance credits can significantly impact your overall application performance. However, by following some best practices and optimizing your usage, you can keep the CPU Credits balance under control.

7.1. Understanding CPU Credit Usage

Every CPU bound operation that runs on your instance consumes a certain amount of CPU credits. Whenever your CPU needs to go beyond the baseline performance, it borrows from this pool of CPU credits. If your workload is consistently overburdening the CPU beyond the baseline, the CPU credit balance will start shrinking.

In severe cases, the balance can go down to zero, which means the instance's CPU will operate at the baseline minimum capacity. This situation, known as CPU Credit Exhaustion, leads to significant performance deficits.

You pay an additional price per CPU credit for exceeding your instance's baseline capacity. Therefore, optimizing CPU Credit usage is also essential to control AWS expenditure.

7.2. Observing the Pattern

The first step towards efficient credit balance management is a keen observation of the usage pattern. You can use Amazon CloudWatch to monitor your usage over a period. CloudWatch metrics such as

CPUCreditUsage and CPUCreditBalance allow you to discern patterns and predict credit balance exhaustion in advance.

Observing patterns in your usage can help you determine what causes the sudden spike in CPU Credit usage. It could be that certain resource-hungry operations run at particular times, or maybe one process consumes most credits.

7.3. Right-Sizing Instances

Right-sizing your instances is an effective strategy to prevent CPU credit exhaustion. This method involves choosing an instance type that fits your workload.

Start with a smaller instance, monitor it for a while, and if CPU utilization remains under the baseline, you have the right instance. If it's exceeding, you should think about moving up the series.

When right-sizing, consider t3 and t4g instances. These instance types include Unlimited mode, which prevents the performance from getting throttled if the CPU credit balance reaches zero by allowing you to borrow credits from the future. However, this incurs a small cost.

7.4. Managing Peak Loads

If your workload's nature is such that it requires a heavy CPU at certain peaks but sub-baseline during other times, Burstable Performance Instances can be an excellent solution. They accumulate CPU credits during low usage times and use them for surges.

This approach saves cost, as the machine won't need to operate at maximum capacity at all times. Also, unlike Fixed Performance Instances which have a constant CPU power, Burstable ones offer flexibility.

7.5. Taking Advantage of Spot Instances

Spot instances offer considerable savings on AWS EC2 expenditure. However, they can be an unstable resource because AWS can reuse these instances with just 2 minutes of notice.

If you have non-critical but resource-heavy background tasks, offloading them to spot instances can be a good strategy – it'll separate your steady application performance from unpredictable CPU Credit consumption.

7.6. Rate Control

Rate Control is a strategy that can prevent CPU Credit exhaustion during large processing jobs. This method involves breaking down a large job into smaller bits. It distributes CPU usage more uniformly over time and hence reduces the risk of credit exhaustion because of a single resource-intensive operation.

For example, if you need to process a large file, you can split it into parts and process them one-by-one. Although this approach may take more time than processing all at once, it prevents your credit balance from plummeting to zero, which in turn, could cause significant disruption to overall performance.

7.7. Using Auto Scaling Groups

If you have fluctuating workloads, Auto Scaling groups can dramatically help in dealing with CPU Credit balance exhaustion. AWS Auto Scaling monitors your applications and adjusts capacity to maintain steady, predictable performance at the lowest possible cost. It can automatically add new instances when there's an increase in workload and terminate them after the peak.

7.8. Limiting Background Processes

Unnecessary or non-essential background operations often consume a significant amount of CPU credits. Therefore, keep a keen eye on your background processes and their priority. You may choose to run these operations on off-peak hours, or better yet, terminate unwanted processes.

7.9. Leveraging the Power of AWS Lambda

For event-driven workloads that may spike CPU usage, consider using AWS Lambda. Since the Lambda functions operate in a stateless manner, they don't sustain CPU Credit balances. They are the ideal candidate for sudden, resource-hungry tasks that might lead to credit exhaustion.

In conclusion, understanding your application's nature and utilizing that knowledge is crucial in avoiding CPU credit exhaustion. Tactics like right-sizing instances, controlling the rate of resource consumption, managing fluctuations, and understanding your CPU Credit usage patterns can go a long way in ensuring efficient and optimized AWS resource use.

Chapter 8. In-depth Guide to Monitoring EC2 Instance Credit Balance

To effectively curb EC2 Instance Credit Balance Exhaustion, the first crucial step is monitoring. Understandably, the process can initially seem overwhelming. But, fret not! This comprehensive guide walks you through, step by step, into the depths of EC2 instance credit balance monitoring.

8.1. Understanding Your EC2 Instance Credit Balance

CPU Credit balance is an integral component of your EC2 instances. It's the 'fuel' that keeps your instances running efficiently. But what exactly are these credits?

In simple words, credits are microscopic units that AWS uses to determine the CPU capacity for burstable performance instances. These instances accumulate CPU credits when idle and consume them when they are active. AWS allots CPU credit balance at the launch and accruals happen per hour, depending on the instance type.

8.1.1. Monitoring Tools

Having outlined what CPU credits are, let's now delve into the tools available for monitoring your EC2 instance credit balance.

Amazon CloudWatch, a monitoring and observability service built for DevOps engineers, developers, site reliability engineers (SREs), and IT managers, is one such useful tool for this task. CloudWatch provides you with data and actionable insights to monitor your applications, understand and respond to system-wide performance changes, optimize resource utilization, and obtain a unified view of operational health.

Specific for our task, the service includes a special metric, `CPUCreditBalance`, which helps you to monitor the CPU credit balance of your instance. This balance is crucial because if your instance's CPU credit balance depletes, it can significantly impact your operations' efficiency.

8.1.2. Viewing Your CPU Credit Balance

To view your CPU credit balance via CloudWatch, follow these steps:

1. Open the CloudWatch console in your AWS Management Console.

2. In the navigation pane, choose Metrics.

3. Choose the EC2 namespace.

4. Scroll down to `Per-Instance Metrics`.

5. Discover the `CPUCreditBalance` metric in the metrics list.

Do remember that this view displays the data in five-minute percentiles.

8.2. Setting Up Alarms for Credit Balance

Now that we know how to view the CPU Credit Balance, the next step is to set up alarms for credit depletion. Alert systems warn when your credits are running low, allowing you to take necessary action before any disruption happens.

To set up CloudWatch alarms for low CPU credit balance:

1. In the CloudWatch console navigation pane, choose Alarms.

2. Choose Create alarm.

3. In `Create Alarm`, select the `EC2 Per-Instance Metrics` namespace.

4. Search for `CPUCreditBalance` and select the respective checkbox.

5. Configure actions according to your preference (e.g., send a notification email when the CPU Credit balance goes below a certain level).

Setting up these alarms allows you to keep track of your credit balances and prevent their exhaustion, ensuring smooth functioning.

8.3. Optimizing Usage

With monitoring in place, the next stage is to optimize usage. AWS itself provides a guideline on how much CPU Credit Balance should be maintained.

For T2 and T3 instances, AWS recommends maintaining a CPU Credit Balance of at least 30% of the initial CPU Credit Balance given at launch. For example, if the instance receives 30 CPU Credits at launch, maintenance of at least 9 CPU Credits is advised.

In case you want to monitor your CPU usage to ensure it is optimized, use the CloudWatch `CPUUtilization` metric, which measures the percentage of CPU usage.

You can also maximize the usage of CPU Credit Balance by:

1. Adjusting your instance sizes: Bigger instances have higher CPU Credit Baselines and earn more CPU Credits per hour.

2. Using T2 Unlimited/T3 Unlimited: These options allow instances to burst beyond the baseline for as long as required, preventing CPU Credit balance depletion.

8.4. Regular Assessments

A crucial practice for effective credit balance management is regular assessments. Continual monitoring and auditing your EC2 instances reveal patterns, allowing you to align your strategies better.

CloudWatch offers options to look at data over various time periods, helping you track trends and deviations over time. Regular assessments also help in understanding the instances' habits.

For instance, if an instance has the pattern of depleting at the same time regularly, it might be due to a background process or a scheduled task. Identifying these processes or tasks allows you to control the depletion and manage your CPU balance better.

Through the careful and thoughtful implementation of monitoring and alerting mechanisms as depicted in this guide, potential crises can be averted and costs can be minimized. Regular monitoring, optimization, and review of the consumption patterns of your EC2 instances are the instruments to long-term, efficient CPU Credit Balance management.

Remember, the digital universe rewards the vigilant. It's time to start monitoring!

Chapter 9. Smart Scaling: Leveraging Auto Scaling and On-Demand Instances

Among the many resources available to enhance EC2 instance performance, Auto Scaling and On-Demand instances have been proven immensely useful. Though straightforward on the surface, there is a wealth of strategic depth behind these tools, capable of optimizing both your resources and costs.

9.1. Understanding Auto Scaling

Auto Scaling, a service offered by AWS, allows users to scale their applications automatically by adjusting EC2 instances up or down, depending on the demand. It ensures that your application maintains peak performance by providing a balanced fleet of EC2 instances, enduring whatever load conditions prevail.

Auto Scaling operates based on plans set by users, which define the desired conditions to trigger the scaling process. When those conditions are met, EC2 automatically scales your resources upward by adding more instances or downward by discarding extra instances, ensuring your application remains healthy and delivers optimal performance, all while keeping your costs in check.

Let's take a simple situation to understand how Auto Scaling works. Suppose you run an e-commerce website which experiences higher traffic during the holiday season, consequently increasing the demand for computing resources. During this time, if you have configured Auto-Scaling, EC2 will automatically add more instances to handle the increased traffic, ensuring your website's performance remains unscathed and customers enjoy a seamless shopping experience. Once the holiday season ends, and traffic diminishes, EC2 will automatically reduce the extra instances, saving unnecessary costs.

Importantly, Auto Scaling is not only useful during traffic spikes but also immensely beneficial during downtime or low traffic periods. Under such conditions, Auto Scaling reduces your instances, conserving costs, ensuring you only pay for what you use.

9.2. Implementing Auto Scaling

Implementing Auto Scaling entails the creation of launch configurations and Auto Scaling groups.

A launch configuration is a template that Auto Scaling uses to launch EC2 instances. When creating a launch configuration, you specify information for the instances such as the ID of the Amazon Machine Image (AMI), the instance type, a key pair, security groups, and block device mapping.

If you've configured the instances to run in a Virtual Private Cloud (VPC), you can also specify a ClassicLink-enabled VPC to which your instances will be linked, a public IP address, or an IP address from an IP address pool.

Next, we have the Auto Scaling group. An Auto Scaling group contains a collection of EC2 instances, which are treated as a logical grouping for the purposes of automatic scaling and management. When you create an Auto Scaling group, you'll need to specify the details for its launch configuration, a maximum and minimum size of the Auto Scaling group, the desirable capacity when it's created, and Network Load Balancer, if any.

Once linked with a spot fleet, Auto Scaling groups can also allow organizations to launch and manage a collection of Spot Instances, On-Demand Instances, and RIs to maintain highly available applications while significantly reducing costs.

9.3. On-Demand Instances

In addition to Auto Scaling, AWS offers the option of On-Demand Instances. These instances let you pay for compute capacity by the hour, or seconds, depending on the instances you run. No long-term commitments or upfront payments are needed. This way, you can scale capacity up or down seamlessly depending on the demands of your application and only pay the specify hourly rate for the instances you use.

On-Demand Instances are ideal for users who prefer the low cost and flexibility without any upfront payment or long-term commitment. They are beneficial for applications with short-term, irregular workloads that cannot be interrupted, or for applications being developed or tested on EC2 for the first time.

9.4. Smart Scaling Strategy

A smart scaling strategy revolves around leveraging both Auto Scaling and On-Demand Instances effectively. AWS provides an enormous benefit of customizing your cloud services as per your usage and demands. Balancing your usage by utilizing both these services can significantly optimize your costs and enhance your application's performance.

For example, you can use On-Demand Instances to handle the normal, everyday workload of your application, ensuring it runs smoothly during typical operations scenarios. Combined with Auto Scaling, during peak load conditions, you can automatically provision additional instances to support the increased demand. Once the peak load subsides, the Auto Scaling function can wind down the extra instances, leaving only the On-Demand Instances running to handle the normal workload.

By effectively leveraging these AWS capabilities, you can not only curb EC2 instance CPU credit balance exhaustion but also ensure efficient performance, increased uptime, and cost optimization on AWS. This strategy allows you to transform cloud computing complexities into your advantage, making sure your operations maintain the right balance between demand, performance, and costs. As you delve deeper into these concepts, you'll unveil more ways to effectively manage your EC2 instances, becoming a virtuoso in AWS cloud computing.

Chapter 10. Building Resiliency: Solutions for High Availability Applications

Building robust, resilient systems is a key goal for any successful cloud operation. These systems should be able to maintain operations even under stress and recover expediently when stressors cause failures. To achieve this, high availability needs to be a consideration right from the architecture design stage. It's not an add-on but a fundamental building block. High availability ensures your applications are always accessible, providing users with uninterrupted service and a positive user experience.

10.1. Understanding High Availability

High Availability (HA) in the context of Amazon EC2 instances refers to the practice of ensuring your applications stay operational, have near-zero downtime, and can seamlessly cope with component failures. The goal is straightforward: Ensure that your end-users can access your services without interruptions, even if specific nodes or services within your architecture fail.

In the cloud and particularly in the AWS ecosystem, achieving high availability typically involves deploying applications or services across multiple Availability Zones (AZs) in a particular AWS Region. Doing so ensures that if one Availability Zone experiences an issue, your application or service can continue operating unaffected using instances in another AZ.

10.2. The Role of EC2 Instance Types in High Availability

AWS offers different types of EC2 instances, each tailored to meet different performance requirements. For instance, Compute Optimized instances are ideal for compute-intensive tasks, Memory Optimized instances are suitable for memory-intensive tasks, and so on. However, T2 and T3 instances are common choices for cost-effectiveness, especially for non-production environments or small-scale applications.

T2 and T3 instances come with a baseline performance and a mechanism to burst above that baseline using CPU Credits. Still, this model can potentially result in performance degradation if the CPU credit balance gets exhausted.

10.3. Scaling: A Key Strategy for High Availability

Scaling is one of the most effective strategies to increase high availability and prevent EC2 instance CPU credit balance exhaustion. There are two ways to scale – vertically (add more computational power to your existing EC2 instances), horizontally (add more EC2 instances to disperse the workload).

With vertical scaling, there is always an upper limit— moving from a t2.micro to a t2.medium will give you only a finite performance boost. Once you hit the ceiling of the available instance types, you've maxed out, and vertical scaling becomes non-viable.

Horizontal scaling is more flexible. It involves adding more instances to manage the load and maintain optimal performance. In AWS terms, this strategy is called Auto Scaling, a service that allows you to maintain application availability automatically and scale your

Amazon EC2 capacity up or down according to conditions you define.

10.4. Implementing High Availability with Auto Scaling and Load Balancing

AWS Auto Scaling allows you to set conditions for when you want to scale in (reduce capacity) and scale out (increase capacity). You can define these according to your business needs, such as the time of day or CPU usage rates.

An example of an auto-scaling strategy is to increase the number of EC2 instances when the CPU credit balance dips below a threshold level. This strategy ensures that even under heavy load, your application won't suffer from performance degradation due to exhausted CPU credits.

While Auto Scaling handles adjusting capacity, AWS Elastic Load Balancing distributes incoming application traffic across multiple targets, such as EC2 instances. It can handle varying workloads efficiently, and combined with Auto Scaling, it significantly contributes to high availability, fault tolerance, and better user experience.

10.5. Monitoring and Alarm: The Pillars of Proactive Management

Achieving and maintaining high availability requires ongoing monitoring. AWS CloudWatch provides the toolset to track your applications, collect and analyze data, set alarms, and react to changes in your AWS resources.

For EC2 instances, particularly T2 or T3 types, watching for the credit balance is crucial. You can create CloudWatch Alarms to keep track of this metric and notify you when it drops below a certain threshold.

10.6. Designing for Failure at the Outset

While it's impossible to predict every failure that might occur, it's essential to plan for them. Here are few strategies for building a fault-tolerant system:

1. Redundancy: Maintain sufficient redundancy in your system. This could be database replication, running multiple instances of the same service, etc.

2. Backups and fast recovery: Regularly back up your data and have a streamlined process for restoring it quickly if required.

3. Loose coupling: Decouple your services as much as possible. The failure of one service should not impact another disproportionately.

4. Graceful degradation: Design your system so that if a component failure occurs, the user experience is degraded minimally.

Being aware of potential obstacles and knowing how to tackle them can help accomplish high availability for your applications. The goal is to build a robust system while optimizing the use of CPU credits efficiently to prevent exhaustion. AWS provides a vast array of services and strategies to assist you in achieving high availability—giving you the means to provide your users with a seamless, uninterrupted service.

Chapter 11. Pulling It All Together: Towards Efficient EC2 Credit Balance Management

To holistically manage your EC2 Instance Credit Balance, you need to get a firm grasp on multiple facets. In this section, we integrate all the core concepts, tools, and strategies discussed so far and propose an approach to EC2 Credit Balance Management.

11.1. Understanding The Baseline

Before embarking on any optimization journey, understand your current state, or the baseline. In the case of EC2 Credit Balance, this includes identifying the workloads running on your EC2 instances. Understand their nature - periodic or persistent, intensive or light, consistent or inconsistent. Evaluating the utilization patterns can offer insights into whether you have instances that are underused (indicating overprovisioning or incorrect instance type) or constantly maxing out their credit balance (indicating underprovisioning or incorrect instance type).

Also, account for the peak loads and their frequency. If these occur infrequently, you might benefit from burstable instances to cater to these sporadically high demands effectively.

In addition, keep track of your current costs, instances' performance, and any issues like application slowness or problems that arise due to EC2 Credit Balance exhaustion.

11.2. Monitoring And Alerts

Monitoring is the cornerstone of any optimization effort. Use CloudWatch, AWS's monitoring tool, for in-depth insights about your CPU Credit Balance. CloudWatch offers a feature to set alarms when certain thresholds are breached. For instance, you could set an alarm when the CPU Credit Balance falls below a particular level. This allows you to react proactively and adjust your instance sizes or types before the situation escalates into a full-blown application performance issue.

11.3. Autoscaling And Load Balancing

Autoscaling is a powerful feature available on AWS. It allows you to scale your resources up or down, depending on your workload's need. However, this should not be used in isolation but along with load balancing. Load balancing ensures that the incoming network traffic is efficiently distributed across multiple EC2 Instances in real time. The use of both Autoscaling and Load Balancing can ensure efficient use of your instances and reduce the risk of exhausting your CPU Credit Balance.

11.4. Selecting The Right EC2 Instance Type

Your choice of EC2 instance can make a significant difference in how fast your CPU Credit Balance depletes. Burstable performance instances (T2, T3, T3a series), for instance, provide a baseline performance with the capability to burst above the baseline using CPU Credits. If your workloads are not continuously high, these instance types could be a cost-effective choice. However, be mindful to avoid reaching a zero CPU Credit Balance, which could lead to throttling, causing your applications to slow down.

Meanwhile, for heavy, constant loads, choosing instances with dedicated performance (like M5, C5 series) could be more appropriate. Though a more expensive option, it ensures your operations never face credit balance exhaustion.

11.5. Regular Updates And Review

The final step is to make your EC2 Credit Balance Management a continuous process. Regularly review your instances, performance, and costs. AWS frequently introduces newer instance types with better performance and cost characteristics. Staying current with these changes could help further optimize your AWS resources.

In conclusion, effective EC2 Credit Balance Management requires a multi-pronged approach. It involves understanding your current situation, configuring monitoring and alerts correctly, using tools like auto-scaling and load balancing efficiently, and choosing an appropriate EC2 instance type, all while ensuring regular revisions and updates. By doing so, you'll ensure your operations run smoothly, cost-effectively, and above all, devoid of unpleasant surprises caused by CPU Credit Balance exhaustion. Keep optimizing!